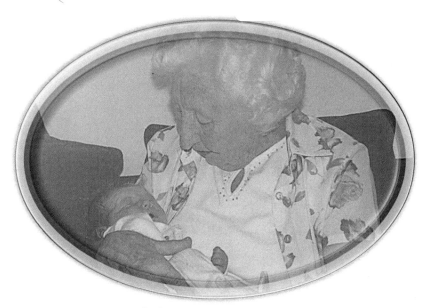

For Kate's great grandchildren

Kate, Harry, Emily, William and Thomas

and

all the future generations to come

With Best Wishes
Judy Chapman
(neé Cooper)

Cover design by Nigel Battley & Judy Chapman

Book design by Judy Chapman & Nigel Battley

Original script by Kathleen Florence Cooper

Additional script by Judy Marion Chapman (nee Cooper)

Published by Bats Publications Ltd.

161 Stockhouse Lane, Surfleet, Spalding, Lincolnshire. PE11 4AT

www.batcaveenterprises.com

First print 2020

Printed by Book Printing UK www.bookprintinguk.com
Remus House, Coltsfoot Drive, Peterborough, PE2 9BF

Originally printed in Great Britain

This publication contains references transcribed from original notes made at the time of events. Although every precaution has been taken in the preparation of this book, the publisher and author assume no responsibility for errors or omissions. Neither is any liability assumed for damages resulting from the use of the information contained herein.

ISBN 978 1 912630 01 1

<u>KATHLEEN</u>

A Twentieth-Century Tale

"A treasured item of Jewellery"

made by Kathleen's Maternal Grandfather
William Grimshaw (pg. 2)

KATHLEEN

A Twentieth-Century Tale

Kathleen Florence (known by her family as Kath) was born in Leytonstone, Essex, in the spring of 1916, in the middle of the Great War.

When in her seventies, the realisation she knew little about her grandparents prompted Kath to start writing notes about her own life story, determined future generations of her family would know theirs.

The following pages describe, in her own words and style (including punctuation), her life as found scribed in several exercise books, penned in her neat handwriting, an example of which can be seen on the cover.

Early Life

My parents, Florrie and Henry, were married on July the 1ˢᵗ 1915 at Leytonstone Wesleyan church. I've no idea what Mum wore but assume that Dad was in uniform as he volunteered to join the Army at the beginning of WWI in 1914 and was then a sergeant in the Royal Field Artillery.

My Mother (maiden name, Grimshaw) was born in Hackney and worked as a machinist when she left school at the age 14 - everlasting proof as she had a machine needle pierce her finger at the base of the nail which was permanently disfigured (she used to tell me it was healed by wrapping a cabbage leaf round it).

My mother - Florence

She was born in 1890 and had four brothers and one sister. Will, born in 1886, who went to Australia in WW1 and joined the army. He later went to Passenda in USA and was the founder of a typewriter company - apparently became quite important judging from his obituary notices. Another brother was born in 1889 but died a little later, a sister was born in 1893 but died within a few years. Bert, who you met when he came over from America, was born, I think, about 1892. He married a French woman during or soon after WW1 but I think he was a bit of a lad - brought Claire over to England when I was very young then went back to Paris but things didn't work out.

They went to America and had a grocery store but the marriage broke up - don't think they were ever divorced - no children - but from about 1930 he lived with a widow called Dot and her family who I stayed with in New Jersey on my visit in 1967.

There was another brother who seemed to have been a black sheep, name of Arthur who lived in Kingston[1]. My Mother must have been in touch with him as I think he had two daughters - one occasionally stayed with us at Leytonstone.

Grandad Grimshaw is only a vague memory. He was a skilled craftsman, an ivory carver who died when I was about 5. I do remember going to the hospital with my Mum, having to watch while she filled in several papers and then watching the porter pull open a large drawer for her to look in.

I was told years later that it was actually the cabinet containing his body which she was identifying but I was never told he was dead. Attitudes as to what was spoken about to children those days were very peculiar. Of his wife, my Grandmother, I have even less memory. Her maiden name was Fitchew and I

Grandma & Grandad Grimshaw

know she remarried to a man named Souter who was a forest warden or gamekeeper in the woods at Coldharbour near Dorking and vaguely remember visiting her in a lovely little cottage in the middle of the woods. She died in 1937 and I remember Mum going on her own to the funeral. I can only assume that the family did not get on well with each other.

The only one of the older generation with whom I had a good deal of contact was my Great Aunt Mary, a smashing person with sparkling dark brown eyes like shiny buttons. At one time she was

---

(1) Judy has since made contact with 2 descendants of Arthur - his grandson David who was put up for adoption as a child and knew nothing of his Grimshaw relatives, and Arthur's daughter Margaret from his 3rd marriage who, although a first cousin of Kate's, is the same age as Judy.

a Salvation Army lassie. I seem to have lost the photo of her in her old fashioned SA bonnet with the ribbon frill. She was great fun and stayed with us a great deal after she was widowed. Later she moved to Fishergate near Brighton where she owned three little Flint cottages on the edge of the coast and I spent many holidays with her right up to the time I married - also used to go down straight from the office to spend the evening with her (it used to cost me 6 shillings, or 30 pence from London Bridge Station and took 59 minutes). When she died just before the War she left me £25, untold riches in those days when my wages were only about £3, but I seem to be running ahead of myself.

My Father was born in 1888 at 9 Barclay Road, Leytonstone - a twin, the last children of James and Emily. I always thought he was born at number 17 but must have moved there later. He was one of 9 children, one died young. The oldest, Jim, was already married and living in Durban South Africa about the time my Father Henry and his twin sister Nell were born, quite a wide spread out family. The others of the family were Bob, Albert, Sue, Jess and Emily so you can see why I have so many cousins, at least 18 all together just from my father's side alone.

My father - Henry

My paternal Grandma was very tiny, about 4' 10" but she was very sharp. Had to be in control I suppose with such a large family. Grandad started the family Builders and Decorators business that was later taken over before the 1914-18 war by three of the sons, Henry, Bob and Albert and the Grandparents then bought several acres of land in the middle of Canvey Island and built a large house that I remember so well.

They were among the first of the permanent dwellers of the Island where they died within 3 weeks of each other in 1923.

I bitterly regret not knowing anything about the years before my parents' marriage. Mother became companion to a Miss Gough, a wealthy spinster who lived alone in a large house in Bushwood, Leytonstone, and I would love to know how Mum and Dad met. I can only assume that maybe he did some decorating for Miss Gough and that's how they met. Dad went into the Army in 1914, the only one of the brothers to join up. After less than one month he got one stripe and later two within 5 months and was eventually promoted to Battery Sergeant Major.

Their first home was a half house at 18 Barclay Road right opposite the family business builders yard. I was born there 10 months later. It was a home delivery. Whether Dad was in England or not I don't know, in fact I was very surprised to learn that he spent a great deal of the War in Egypt, Gallipoli and Palestine which in those days of very little travel must have seemed a terrifically frightening experience. Of course, as he was in the Artillery he was mounted and I find it so difficult to visualise him spending all the War years on a horse. I

Baby me and my Mum

have his Army discharge documents and see that he was finally "out" in April 1919 after 5 years of service for which he received the mean sum of £29 gratuity.

He was injured somehow during the War and several years later he suffered from a terrible abscess on the spine which nearly cost him his life as it was of course before the days of penicillin. He was never comfortable with me, seemed to be afraid of spoiling me as the only child.

~ 4 ~

I suppose it was while Dad was overseas that Mum travelled away from Leytonstone with me. Whether there was a fear of air raids on London I don't know but at one time we were living at Framlingham in Suffolk and later near Bexhill.

Kathleen aged 2

I have no memories of his return from the War but my first recollection of him recalls his irritation when, on lifting me to board a tram in Leytonstone High Street, he discovered that the whitening off my little white shoes has rubbed off on his navy blue Melton overcoat.

My childhood was typical of those days I suppose - strict obedience to, and respect for, my parents. Mother was devoted to Dad, her whole life was centred on him and nothing was allowed to distress or disturb him. Life was run to a strict timetable and woe betide anything that upset it. He had been brought up in the strict Wesleyan tradition and Mum had changed over from C of E on marriage. From my very young days I had to attend Sunday School and Chapel 3 times on Sundays and any social life revolved around choir practice (they were both members but I managed to keep out of it), Guild and other activities.

At the age of 5 I went to Kirkdale Road Infants School and about that time we moved to a fairly large house at 44 Woodville Road. I don't remember anything about the move except that I went off to school in the morning from Barclay Road and went home at lunchtime to the new house. It had 2 lounges, 4 bedrooms, a dining room, kitchen and scullery with a large conservatory leading off the lounges where I spent a great deal of my time. It contained a large grape vine which bore magnificent bunches of black grapes. I kept a cage of brown and white mice in this conservatory. They really were my companions. My friend Phyllis lived in the same road.

I was a lonely child and read a terrific amount, usually while sitting in my favourite rocking chair, and was always worrying my parents for a dog but told "no". Then we looked after a neighbours terrier puppy while the young wife went away to have a baby, but she died, together with her newborn twins, I think as a result of tripping over the dog, and that's how I had Bodger who was with us until I got married.

Piano lessons and practice daily were one of my trials. I also had to enter singing contests which I hated as nerves usually got the better of me although I won several awards so could not have been too bad. A great deal was expected of me. I was always expected to be top of the class and there was an air of disappointment at home if I did not keep up this standard. No wonder I developed such nervous habits and twitches, even my Aunts told my Father that he was expecting too much of me but I was always expected to aim for perfection. It was unfortunate that Mother had no more children, in fact I do remember being taken to look in pram shop windows and the idea being put to me that perhaps I would be having a brother or sister but apparently Mum had a miscarriage and she told me years later that although she would have liked more children she had suffered some internal damage at my birth which was a forceps delivery and accounts for my slightly crooked face that was a great source of worry to me in my teens.

School Days

Education in those days was very different compared with modern systems. Entry to advanced education at High or Grammar Schools was by fee paying, which seemed confined to professional people only or the much fought for "scholarship" places of which only one or two were granted to each Elementary school. Those who were not clever enough stayed at their first and only school until the age of 14 when they left to take up any form of work for very low pay.

The day of the Scholarship exam was nerve wracking. Only a chosen few were allowed to sit for it and we spent all day at the High School, suffering awe and fright. On the day the results were due to be announced I was almost too scared to go to school and when I found a place at the High School was not for me was almost afraid to go home to tell my parents. Such a high prestige was placed on going to the High but Scholarship girls did not have too happy a time as they were looked down on by the fee paying students, even though they were possibly a lot brighter than the elite who had only had to pass a simple entrance exam.

At that time, 1926, Essex Educational Authorities had the bright idea of opening what were called "Central" schools for pupils who were bright but had not gained scholarships and I was fortunate to gain a place in the first very modern co-educational school called "Thomas Hood Central".

Once again I started off at a disadvantage as my Father, who could have taken his annual summer holiday at any time, chose it so I missed the first week at a fresh school so that I missed out on the introduction to French, Algebra, Geometry etc and in my 5 years there felt that I never really caught up, and to crown it all, left-handedness seemed to be considered a sin. The shorthand master made life very unpleasant for me as he said I was "pushing" against the paper instead of flowing with it and after many attempts to make me change over to right handedness the teacher gave up in despair and I was made to feel it was a disgrace. Thank goodness teachers are more enlightened these days.

Working Life

From the age of about 15 my parents tried to map out a future career for me. I wanted to train for nursing but this idea was squashed as nurses had a very rough life in those days. Dad wanted me to take the Civil Service entrance exam as that was classed as a good steady job with pension prospects. As I was due to start work in 1932 when the Depression was at its worst I suppose jobs in the Post Office and such like were certain security but I wanted to do something different so suggested that I might become a Comptometer operator. Comptometers were the most up to date calculators at that time and the operators were the elite in London offices and could command far higher wages than ordinary office workers. The training school was in Aldwych in London, the diploma course was for 3 months and the fee was £3 3shillings (£3.15) a week - plus my train fares daily had to be paid.

I had no idea of my Father's financial position and was led to believe that great sacrifices had to be made to pay for this training so once again pressure was put on me to succeed. Fortunately I did well, gained my full diploma in the given time and was ready to start in my first job. This was with a textile company in St Paul's Churchyard where I earned 30/- (£1.50) a week out of which I had to give my parents half then pay for my season ticket to London, lunches and clothes! All on 15/- a week and yet I never seemed to be hard up, which just shows how money values have changed.

After a year I left and took a job in Leyton, much nearer home with a firm that made cakes, but left after about 6-8 months. I never did manage to explain to my parents why I made the change as personal matters were so difficult to mention but nowadays the carryings on of the two fairly young office managers would be referred to as sexual harassment!

From there I entered the very sober world of a very large Assurance Company - a prestige job with the Atlas Assurance in Cheapside, but Oh! so boring. Working hours were good - from 9.45-4.45 for a 5 day week and 9.45-12.30 on Saturdays so I was able to avoid the rush hour travel. Life was very strict; we had to wear long sleeves, business like clothes meaning dark colours and respectable lengths, hats and gloves. On Saturdays we were allowed to wear less somber clothes and the men were allowed to wear tweeds instead of business suits. Just imagine such restrictions being placed on office workers today, but at that time we saw nothing wrong with it, were just thankful to be in such a prestigious job where we were in the centre of so much of interest. Our office was on the corner of Cheapside and King Street, the road leading to the Guildhall, so were able to see all the ceremonials such as visiting Royalty when they occurred and the Lord Mayors Show when I was able to wave to Eddie who was in the parade. But more of that later.

When I left in 1938 to marry I think my salary was £3 a week. The job could be extremely boring at times and I now feel great sympathy with people who have to do soul destroying office or factory jobs.

The Coopers

So far I have not mentioned the Cooper side of the family. Horace and Agnes Cooper (Eddies parents) were managers of a wine merchants business in Leytonstone High Road right opposite the Wesleyan Chapel my family were involved with. Horace's father (Eddies grandfather) was a farrier and blacksmith with his anvil near The Green Man hotel in Leytonstone - it's amazing to realise that horses were shod just 8 miles from the centre of London but of course when I was young and then in my teens, deliveries of bread, milk, greengroceries etc were made by horse and cart.

The Coopers were not a close happy family and Mr and Mrs C were certainly not a devoted couple. Eddie, the oldest, born in 1912 spent his early school days near Portsmouth. His father was in the Catering Corps in the Army in the first War and I understand that they came to London when Joan was born in 1917, followed by Frank in 1919. They lived over the shop and I can never remember any family gatherings as one or the other always seemed to be on duty in the shop. Frank left home as soon as he could to join the Royal Navy at a very early age and Joan was an apprenticed hairdresser.

Courtship and Marriage

I first remember Eddie when we were at Junior School - he was the "big boy" who blew the Last Post on his bugle on Armistice Day when we all assembled around the War Memorial, and now realise that for anyone as unmusical as him it was amazing that he hit the right notes! He was very involved with the Boys Brigade and was an enthusiastic member of the band. I was in the Girls Brigade and for years our lives revolved around these societies, we had a great many friends and were involved with so many activities, summer camps, displays at the Royal Albert Hall etc.

From the age of about 13 or 14 we always seemed to be together (or falling out as often happened). When he was 15 he started work as an office boy at the Bentwood Chair Works at Dalston where he cycled daily, but he always hankered after the Army so at 18 or 19 he joined the Royal West Kent Regiment (The Buffs) and was posted to their depot at Canterbury. I'm afraid he was sadly disillusioned with Army life and after a few months pleaded with his Father to buy him out. In those days this was a very expensive thing to do but his Dad was very good about it even though he really couldn't afford to do so.

After coming out of the Army he looked ghastly, shaven head etc - but soon recovered and got a job with the National Cash Register Co, then in Tottenham Court Road but later transferred to new premises in Marylebone Road where he was very happy in the shipping department, sometimes having to check goods in at The Docks or Croydon Airport (no Heathrow in those pre-war days),
He still hankered after Army life though and in 1932 joined the Territorial Army. As a London office worker he was able to join the famous City of London Yeomanry RHA, the Rough Riders. The attraction was the horses as they were still a mounted Battery and each week he went riding at St John's Wood, summer camps at Aldershot and Salisbury, and ceremonials including riding annually in the Lord Mayors Show which I mentioned earlier. I must say he looked very fetching in full dress uniform and even in normal khaki with riding breeches and Sam Brown - long before the days of battle dress.

I do wish you had known Eddie in those pre-war days, a very different person to the quiet withdrawn person you grew up with. That's what war does for some unfortunately.

Our way of living in the pre-war days was very different as of course there was no TV. In fact my first introduction to radio was when I was 6 in 1922. In most households there was at least one enthusiast who had made their own "cats whisker" crystal sets which we listened to through headphones. I was at a friends house one day when the father stood the headphones in a pudding basin and we were all able to hear the distorted sound of Uncle Mac and Children's Hour. Unforgettable.

In our teens Eddie and I went to the cinema twice most weeks - not a bit like they are now. Sometimes we would queue for at least an hour but what moneys-worth we got when we finally took our seats in those palatial buildings that were the picture houses of those days. For 1/6 (7.5p) we always enjoyed an "A" film, a "B" film, newsreel, travel film or suchlike and a first class live stage show, in all a programme of anything up to 4 hours.

About once a month we went to a theatre to see such shows as The Crazy Gang, Max Miller or the elaborate musicals like the Ivor Novello Shows, White Horse Inn, Desert Song, Jill Darling etc.

Each Sunday morning Eddie would call for me at about 8 o'clock and we would either walk about 10 miles or take out skiffs on the local lake and row for about an hour. On Saturday afternoons we played badminton but I was not very keen on that as I was never very good at, or interested in, any kind of sport.

During the Winter we often went to dances in London (although Eddie never could master the footwork). These were very posh affairs, full evening dress, long gowns, long gloves, a full length black velvet cloak - don't forget we went up to London (only about 9 miles) by train - would look very odd nowadays but it was the norm then as we didn't have cars.

Kath & Eddie

We got engaged on my 21st birthday, bought a diamond and sapphire ring at Bravingtons and I had a party for about 60 in a hall at Woodford but it was a bit of a disaster and I didn't enjoy it. Had it really for my parents sake.

Most of our friends at Leytonstone bought houses no further away than Woodford or Loughton but we decided to go house-hunting across the other side of London so long as the travel was convenient for Town. Our first search was at Kenton but the prices were too high for our income as in those days (1938) only the husband's earnings could be considered for the mortgage. An estate agent suggested that some new property at Carpenders Park, near Watford, would be of more interest to us so we looked, decided the area was very pleasant and countrified so went ahead with plans. The St Meryl Estate was in its early stages, we just had to choose a plot and the type of premises we wanted and it could be built in 3 weeks! (By the way, this small estate was made famous by Leslie Thomas as the basis of his book "Tropic of Ruislip" as he knew the area very well). A house would have cost £525 but we wanted a bungalow and chose the

plans for one half way up a hill that would cost £575[2] Dad generously offered to pay the deposit for a wedding present (£25) so we went ahead with plans to marry on May 28th 1938.

Weddings were not the elaborate affairs they are nowadays, simply because most people's financial positions were very different. Eddie was earning £4.00 per week at that time, rising to £4.50 a few months later and as no woman was expected to, or in some cases not allowed to stay on at work after marriage, I had to make do with temporary work when I could get it to help out cash wise and even then I was not allowed to use my married name, sometimes having to remove my wedding ring. At one time we had considered having a full military wedding but financially that was out of the question so we went to the other extreme and tied the knot at the Methodist Church at 9 o'clock in the morning. At the last minute I nearly changed my mind and at a quarter to 9 started to change the ribbon on my hat to give myself a few more minutes of thinking time! What consternation I could have caused that day.

I wore a tailored navy suit bought at C&A for £5.50, white blouse and navy halo hat. Shoes were bought at Dolcis only the day before for 19/11d. I really did leave things to the last minute.

After a very short service - no music - we (Eddie, his Mother - not father - my parents and me) went in a large hired limousine to Lyons Corner House in Oxford Street for breakfast and then to Liverpool Street where we got a train to Thaxted for a weekend as Eddie was back to work on the Monday morning. I guess this all sounds very odd to you when you think of the elaborate and expensive wedding preparations nowadays.

---

[2] Equivalent to £38,956 at today's values. A similar bungalow in Carpenders Park was recently on Rightmove at £445,000

The following weekend was Whitsun so we, together with about four other couples, went to Worthing where we took over a cottage for a week as we had done with these friends several times before so shared our "honeymoon" with them.

Once I was off their hands my parents decided to make changes. Dad bought out his share of the business and purchased a decorators business of his own at Snodland near Maidstone where they moved to in December 1938.

The War Years

Meanwhile, within a few months of our wedding the first war scares became apparent and as a Territorial Eddie was mobilised in September but Chamberlin signed the Munich Agreement with Hitler so the call-up lasted only a few weeks although from then on we guessed that it was only a matter of time before war became a reality.

In the August Eddie went off to his annual Territorial camp - I think it was held at St Agnes in Cornwall that year - and was once again mobilised, this time for real, so never really returned from camp but was sent straight on to Tilbury. Thus began very eventful 6 years when our lives changed completely. None of you will ever understand or even imagine what it was really like to have a chunk of your life dominated by excitement, horror, day to day fear of the unknown, separation - hardly able to plan for the future as we didn't know if there would be a future.

The first few months of the War were very strange. After the initial shock of the unbelievable actually happening life began to settle a bit and Eddie was moved all over Eastern England, mainly around

Essex. He tried to make arrangements for me to join him wherever he was, would phone me and off I'd go, finding myself sleeping in strange places, anything from a good hotel, joining with another wife in a rented house or sleeping on bare boards in an empty house.

Spring 1940 found him stationed at Beer Regis in Dorset which he thought would be a long stay so I rented rooms there for several weeks but when, in May, Churchill and King George VI inspected them we knew they were due to go overseas. Their status had been raised to the newly formed 1st Armoured Division a very elite Company, and had wonderful and powerful new equipment.

The War in Europe was not going too well so it was obvious where they would be going to after the first of many tearful farewells I was to experience, back to Carpenders Park I returned.

Within a week of the Regiment reaching France the Germans overran Europe, resulting in the Dunkirk retreat but the 1st Armoured Division had been sent over to protect the troops who were heading for the beaches by performing a rearguard action and so saving thousands of men. No word was heard of them because obviously there was no postal communication and so began a few anxious weeks awaiting news. I was working at the Peter Jones store in Sloane Square when we learnt that Paris had been taken so had little hope of learning of a safe return.

The Dunkirk evacuation was over but still no word of Eddie or any of his men and I had no idea where he might be. Eventually, about 3 weeks after thinking that the worst had happened he arrived home unexpectedly in a very sorry state, filthy dirty - without any equipment, longing only for a hot bath, and as I took his socks off the skin of his feet peeled off with them. He was a very changed man - would not talk of his experiences except to keep telling me to stay at home if there was a German invasion - a possibility at that awful time - as he had seen some terrible sights in France when the German planes machine gunned and bombed refugees on the roads. He bottled his feelings up too much and would not tell me about his experiences. Unfortunately this seemed to be the turning point in his life and he was never the same again, the lighthearted man I had known for so many years.

He was given several weeks compassionate leave and when he returned to his unit found that out of his Battery of about 250 only 97 had returned - the rest were killed or POWs. He had lost so many of his "mates". I had the dreadful task of visiting grief stricken wives with whom I had been enjoying our time at Beer Regis only a few weeks earlier.

I eventually found that the Rough Riders had been trapped in France and individually tried to get back to Britain as best they could. Eddie went south, aiming for Spain, ran into more trouble and ended up with a few others at Brest where he hid up until a small ship picked them up and after an eventful journey landed him at Plymouth. The whole affair was a shambles - all of their new equipment, guns, lorries, ammunition etc had to be destroyed and those who returned came back with nothing.

After a week or so of compassionate leave Eddie had to report to Camberley for regrouping and I spent a few weeks in a rather classy hotel but the next move was to Brackley in Surrey where I rented a room but travelled backwards and forward to Carpenders Park. All this time I was not bone idle as I was still on the agencies' books for temporary work anywhere in Southern England - taking my Comptometer to strange places for anything from one day to two weeks - mainly doing the firms wages or stocktaking. I had regular quarterly sessions at both Guildford and Maidstone Gas Companies and did a spell at an aircraft firm at Reading where we had so many air raid warnings that I seemed to spend the week working in underground shelters on their airfield. I was in digs at Reading but used to often go across to Camberley at night, often escorted to the bus by a policeman!

Later that year I was sent to John Lewis in Oxford Street for 2 weeks so travelled from Carpenders Park daily but one Monday I arrived to find Oxford Street had been badly bombed and John Lewis shop had been severely damaged so back to home I went, another job gone.

In the late summer the Battery was moved to Wonersh, about 6 miles from Guildford and Eddie phoned me at Carpenders Park to say he thought they were going to be there for quite a long time - he had been offered the chance to rent half a cottage so did I want to go. I jumped at the chance, put the bungalow in an agent's hands for renting out furnished, soon got a customer as people were looking for living accommodation in reasonably safe areas and moved to Wonersh, not realising that it would be my home for 2 years and so much would happen there.

The following months were lived on a "high". Eddie, by then promoted to Battery Sergeant Major, was stationed in a nearby Manor House called Chinthurst and owned by the Governor of Sarawak, Lord Inchcape but he slept out most nights at our cottage. About half a dozen of us would pile into a car belonging to a very wealthy young gunner and we would dash off to London or Reading for a meal or show, quite crazy but don't forget we were young and making the most of every day, not knowing what might be ahead.

The War was about at its worst in 1940 following the collapse of Europe and invasion by the Germans was a very real possibility.

Then in September the trouble really started, to be known later as The Battle of Britain although it was really The Battle for Britain.

Eddies sister Joan and Ralph had fixed their wedding for September 7th[3] and little did we know what a historic day that would be. I was back at Carpenders Park for some reason and went on my own to Leytonstone as Eddie was on full alert so couldn't get leave. Half way through the marriage service at St Margaret's Church the sirens sounded and there was a terrible noise of aircraft and guns. We all had to go down to the crypt to finish the service and stay down there for ages and when eventually the all clear sounded we could hardly believe our eyes; never in my life did I expect to see bodies floating down on parachutes and utter chaos with the air filled with smoke. We learned later that about 300 German bombers and about twice as many escorting fighters had flown up the Thames to bomb the City and East End, aiming for Woolwich, the Docks and the City.

That evening the newlyweds, who had taken a flat in Cricklewood, and myself tried to get across to North West London but all the routes into London and the stations were closed. We eventually got to Dalton, about 4 miles, mainly by walking, somehow got into a train going to Watford and sat in an unmoving blacked out train for a long time, eating wedding cake!

When I eventually arrived at Carpenders Park the sight from the hill was unbelievable - London really was ablaze, visible from 20 miles away.

I had some very eventful trips between Carpenders Park and Wonersh, often having to make trips around London when the main line stations were closed due to bomb damage and often had to

---

(3) September the 7th 1940 is recognised as being the first day of the blitzkreig over London which continued until May 1941

spend time in rather horrible air raid shelters but the funny thing is that we never seemed to feel fear, would watch dog-fights overhead almost as entertainment. Don't forget we were young then - in our early 20's and had accepted war as part of our lives.

In the Spring of 1941 I was thrilled to bits to find that at last I was pregnant. Looking back I realise that it must seem as though we were mad wanting to have a baby in wartime but as we had no idea how long the War was likely to last we couldn't wait forever and life was going along quite pleasantly for us at that time.

Unfortunately fate stepped in once again because as soon as the pregnancy was confirmed Eddie came home one day with news he hardly dared tell me - they had suddenly been told that they were due to go overseas.

We went up to the Cumberland Hotel at Marble Arch to spend his embarkation leave but the first night there was an air raid on London so the next day we set off for Torquay where we spent 10 days. On our return we said our final fond farewells in June as Eddie went off to Wiltshire prior to going overseas but suddenly the Army changed its plans and home he came again. Once again came the final partings, this time for good, and the last sight he saw of me as I waved the Battery off from a little village station was of a rather bulky 5 month pregnant me.

We thought and hoped that they were off to the Far East but after several weeks he wrote from Durban so we guessed that they were heading for the Middle East. By the time the baby was due they were settled in Egypt - it was no joke having a baby on my own but even worse for Eddie as I later learned it was about 3 weeks later when, out in the desert, he received the cable telling him of Jill's arrival.

Being on my own I had to rely on the owners of the cottage to get me into the hospital at Guildford for the birth but all was well and I stayed living at Wonersh for the next seven or eight months until the people to whom I had let the bungalow moved out so I moved back to Carpenders Park.

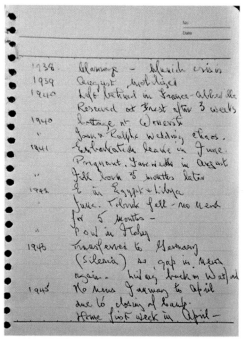

I had just received the frightening War Office telegram in July telling me that Eddie was missing and as you can imagine, the mental strain over the following months was indescribable, hoping for news with each visit from the postman or telephone call. Eventually, 3 or 4 months later I received unofficial news that he was still alive from some nuns in a convent who monitored Vatican Radio each night from which lists of names of prisoners in Italy were read out. This was later confirmed by the Red Cross at the end of November but it had been a very anxious time.

From then onward my days were centered around Jill and the daily appearance of the postman but it was a long time before I had a brief message from a POW camp and life was very hard for both him and me.

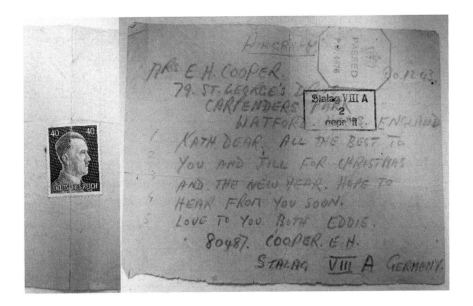

I later learnt that Eddie was captured at Tobruk, was shipped over to Italy and was in various camps from Brindisi up to Naples where he was a POW when Italy capitulated. He unfortunately was in a camp captured by the Germans, had no chance to escape as some of his mates in different camps were lucky enough to do, and was sent off on uncomfortable trains to camps in Germany and eventually Silesia.

For those 3 years 1942-1945 I had to make life for myself and Jill as normal as possible, overcoming the rationing and occasional air raids and horrible flying bombs and naturally I became extremely independent.

When in 1945 it really looked as though we might win the War after all I began to make plans for a wonderful reunion but, as usually happened, nothing turned out as hoped for. At the end of April I had a letter from Belgium to say that Eddie had escaped from the infamous "Death March"[4] across Germany when their guards took them out of the camp (hid up somehow and was involved with Russian POWs but I never did find out the truth of what happened) - would not be home for my birthday on the 29th April but to expect him soon after. By this time I was both sick with excitement but also slightly apprehensive as instead of coming back just to me he had a daughter to get used to and I had no idea what his state of health, both mental and physical, might be and how he could have changed.

MIS-X

GENERAL QUESTIONNAIRE FOR BRITISH/AMERICAN EX-PRISONERS OF WAR.

1. No. _P36033_ RANK _B.S.M._ SURNAME _COOPER._
CHRISTIAN NAMES _EDGAR HORACE_
DECORATIONS _AFRICA STAR - TERRITORIAL EFFICIENCY._

2. SHIP (R.N., U.S.N. or MERCHANT NAVY) _____
UNIT (ARMY) _ROYAL ARTILLERY. - LIGHT AA._
SQUADRON (R.A.F. or A.A.F.) _____

3. DIVISION (ARMY), COMMAND (R.A.F. or A.A.F.) _1ST ARMOURED._

4. DATE OF BIRTH _9.10.12._

5. DATE OF ENLISTMENT _1.3.33._

6. CIVILIAN TRADE OR PROFESSION _CLERK. —_
(OR EXAMINATIONS PASSED WHILE P/W) _ASS. INST. BOOKKEEPERS._

7. PRIVATE ADDRESS _79. ST. GEORGE'S DRIVE. CARPENDERS PARK WATFORD. HERTS. ENGLAND._

8. PLACE AND DATE OF ORIGINAL CAPTURE _23.6.42. TOBRUK._

9. WERE YOU WOUNDED WHEN CAPTURED? _NO._

10. MAIN CAMPS OR HOSPITALS IN WHICH IMPRISONED.

Camp No.	Location	From	Till
P.G. 52.	CHIAVARI.	OCT. '42	SEPT '43
STALAG. VIIIA	GÖRLITZ.	SEPT '43	MAR '44
— 344	LAMSDORF	MAR '44	FEB '45

11. WERE YOU IN A WORKING CAMP? _NO._

Location	From	Till	Nature of Work

12. DID YOU SUFFER FROM ANY SERIOUS ILLNESSES WHILE A P/W? _NO._

Nature of Illness	Cause	Duration

(4) For a history of the "death march" see notes in the back pages

The Soldier Returns

In the middle of the night on the 3rd of May came a phone call from him saying that he had just flown in to Oxfordshire and hoped to be home within 36 hours. Unfortunately my excitement was overshadowed by the appearance of a very spotty daughter. Jill chose just that day to develop German Measles and the misery that went with it. She was quite ill, I sent for the doctor and then it was a toss up who appeared first, Eddie or the doctor or would they arrive on the doorstep together. Bang went my plans of dressing carefully and watching out of the window for him to come up the hill. Eventually the doctor arrived just about half and hour before the returning soldier but by then I was in a state of chaos.

Victory in Europe Day

Early May 1945 was a very strange time. We had all been eagerly awaiting the news that the terrible War was finally over but for some reason it was delayed for days, so it was a great relief when Winston Churchill finally announced that May the 8th would be VE Day.

A street party was planned for our quiet estate but Eddie, who only a few days previously had returned from his terrible years as a Prisoner of War in the infamous camp 344, would not allow three and a half year old Jill, who he'd only just met for the first time, to join in the celebrations. He had too many unhappy memories of lost comrades and experiences that he would never talk about or share with me. As it happened nature decided that we would not join in the celebrations because of Jill's outbreak of German Measles.

Post War

Eddie was a very changed man understandably, considering the rough time he had been through but it was difficult for both of us to readjust. Although his job with the NCR had been kept open for him the prospect of working in the confined space of a London office did not appeal to him at all. He was then offered the chance to transfer to their Dundee office but he refused - said he'd had enough contact with Scotsmen as a POW.

Of course he was not demobilised at once. As with all returning POWs he had to undergo various hospital tests, first of all 3-4 weeks in a hospital at St Albans for mental tests and then to a convalescent hospital at Kempston in Bedfordshire where he read of a job in the local paper for a secretary and accountant to a farmer near Bedford, went after the job while still in uniform, got the job and then came home one weekend to tell me that was what he wanted to do and would I go to look at the cottage we were offered.

I was willing to do anything to make him settled and contented so the following April we moved to the renovated cottage situated in the middle of a cow field. He had been living in the farmhouse since the previous September while the new home was being prepared.

It had been an eventful year in the family. Ed's Dad died very painfully of cancer of the pancreas and some months later his Mother tragically ended her own life. It was only much later that I learnt she suffered from depression, as her younger son Frank did later. Ed's sister Joan and her husband Ralph emigrated to New Zealand on an assisted passage.

My Father sold his business at Snodland and they bought a nice newly built house at Ramsgate.

When we left Carpenders Park (reluctantly on my part I'm afraid to say) I was pregnant and Judy was born 5 months later. I was thrilled to bits at having another girl - much nicer having a baby at home than in hospital. Everything seemed to be going well, especially having a son the next year and the three children had a super start to life living on the farm although it was a very lonely life for me, and Eddie had a pleasant job looking after the accounts of the three farms in Norfolk, Hertfordshire and Bedfordshire as well as exercising the farmer's racehorses, in fact he seemed quite content but after 5 years began to get restless and wanted a place of his own, something that he had had in mind during his years of confinement as a POW. I think also part of the trouble was due to the fact that he had been a Sergeant Major, giving orders to others, he never wanted to take orders from anyone again.

We hadn't got the finances to buy a place and renting was impossible until he heard of the Government controlled Land Settlement[5], applied for a holding, was put on their long waiting list and eventually got short listed. When we were sent to Spalding for an interview I really thought it was the back of beyond. However, after scraping up every penny we could, even selling our beloved car for the large amount required, we were accepted for a five acre holding and so began 34 years which you know all about and which I would rather forget.

My parents soon moved to Westcliff on Sea for some unknown reason and Father, who had suffered various health problems, dropped dead from a coronary at the age of 72. Mother moved to Fulney to a bungalow we found for her near me but she had little desire to live without her husband, suffered two strokes and passed away peacefully in her own home two years later at the age of 72.

---

(5) For a history of the Land Settlement see notes in the back pages

That brings us up to date with Eddies death from emphysema and cancer in 1984 aged 71 and my subsequent sale of the holding that enabled me to purchase my lovely little bungalow at Weston where I am enjoying a very contented life with the knowledge that you all live near and are all happily settled yourselves.

I've had a very exciting and eventful life although it all changed so much after 1945. My regret is that Eddie changed so much. I am sure the modern treatment and understanding that serving soldiers now undergo after being in action would have been of great benefit. He wanted to blank his mind completely to all that had happened, never talked of his experiences and showed no interest in what my life had been like while he was away. You only knew him as a very quiet person but I have memories of him as he was before 1939.

I do hope this account of your family's life will be of some interest to you. I bitterly regret knowing so little of my parents and grandparents lives so hope that one of you will keep this safely for future reference.

I have lived History!

AND NEXT............................

The following two pages show pictures of, and provide information about, a similar Stalag camp to the one Eddie and his comrades were incarcerated within.
Kate brought the pamphlet back with her when visiting the camp many years later.

We have kindly been afforded permission to reproduce this informative pamphlet by the:
City of Luckenwalde Office for Education, Youth and IT Museum

https://www.luckenwalde.de/Stadt/Kultur/Museen/HeimatMuseum/STALAG-III-A-LUCKENWALDE

Web address correct at time of publication

The former prison camp Stalag III A in Luckenwalde 1939-1945

Even before the German invasion of Poland, Luckenwalde was selected as the site for one of the main prison camps planned for the Reich territory. It was designed to accommodate 10,000 people and its construction was to serve as the model for the other camps. On 26 August 1939 the order was given to build the prison camp Stalag III A. By the middle of September 1939 the first Polish prisoners of war had already arrived. Their condition was poor, some of them were insufficient clothing and were undernourished.

Initially, the prisoners were housed in tents measuring 12 x 35 m that were transported from the premises of the Reichssporting in Nuremberg and were made available to the prison camp. This arrangement was initially intended to be provisional, although it became permanent. As soon as new prisoners arrived after a campaign, they were placed in the tents. The tents play a major role in the memories of many prisoners.

Later the prisoners were often held in work parties outside of Luckenwalde. The work parties were spread out over the entire Potsdam administrative district, which today roughly corresponds to the Land Brandenburg.

In the fall of 1939 the number of Polish prisoners that were sent to the Stalag grew to approximately 20,000. One-third remained in the Stalag and began to construct the barracks and the other buildings. The remainder of the prisoners were sent to work exclusively in agriculture during the harvest. They were housed under guard in collective quarters that were built by the prisoners. The barracks were completed in winter, they formed the core of the camp. The entire Stalag complex comprised of approximately 100 buildings, including an infirmary, functional buildings, quarters for the guards and camp personnel, whereas merely one-third of it was planned for housing prisoners. The up to 50 tents that were set

Arrival of Polish prisoners of war (1939)

Construction of the barracks 1939

up after the arrival of the prisoners were located between the barracks and toilet facilities and the perimeter fence and formed the outermost part of the camp. In the early part of the summer of 1940 the Polish prisoners were gradually transferred to the status of civilian workers. They often went kept on at the Armed Forces, the police and not the Armed Forces, were in charge of them and they applied stricter laws. Then the prisoners from the Western Campaign arrived, initially the Dutch and Belgians, who were to only remain in the camp for a short period, for example, the Dutch were released just a few weeks later. The French prisoners who came to Luckenwalde from the summer of 1940 on formed the group that was to characterize the image of the camp.

Nearly 40,000 French prisoners were assigned to the Stalag. In contrast to the Poles they were also put to work in the industry. In the area of Berlin and Brandenburg they became an important workforce of potential of the wartime economy. The number of POWs that were prisoners from Luckenwalde rose at times to more than 30,000.

The administrative apparatus of the camp likened therefore that of a mid-sized city. The town of Luckenwalde only had a population of around 12,000 at the time.

Prisoners of war from Stalag III A in a work detail

From 1940 on Luckenwalde was no longer the only site of an independent prison camp in Brandenburg. In December 1939 Stalag III B, which was approximately the same size, was built in Fürstenberg an der Oder (today Eisenhüttenstadt); Stalag III C followed shortly after in the summer of 1940, being built to the east of the Elbe near in Alt-Drewitz. Berlin was the site of a decentrally structured Stalag III D around the same time, which supplied workers to the industry in and around Berlin in all, over that 130,000 prisoners of war were being held in the Military District III. The French continued to constitute the largest group of prisoners of war in Luckenwalde, as well as in the entire Military District, until the end of the war. Following the path of the battlefields, Serbian prisoners came in 1941 to Luckenwalde, to the end of the year, for example, the remainder of the USSR Soviet prisoners also were sent there.

Whereas the number of Serbian prisoners constantly declined, the number of Soviet prisoners increased greatly until the end of the war. After the change in Italian frontline approximately 16,000 military prisoners came to Luckenwalde within a short period of time in 1943, the minority of which were quickly distributed to other camps. Towards the end of the war British and Polish prisoners as well as the first American and Romanian prisoners were shipped to the camp so that representatives from more than 15 of the countries at war were interned at the Stalag in Luckenwalde during the course of the war.

At the beginning of 1945, when the Red Army reached the Oder river, Stalag III B in Fürstenberg was evacuated. The internees of this camp stopped off along the way for several weeks in Luckenwalde, leading to the camp being utterly overfilled and having catastrophic hygienic conditions. A lustic commander appointed for the camp in the last weeks of the war yet. Fortunately, it was not necessary to defend the camp since the guard troops and officers defected to the west before the Soviet troops marched in.

~ 28 ~

Stalag III A
Luckenwalde

Permanent exhibition on Stalag III A

Heimatmuseum Luckenwalde
Markt 11
14943 Luckenwalde
Germany
Tel: +49 (3371) 61339
Fax: +49 (3371) 632112
E-mail: kultur@luckenwalde.de
Internet: www.luckenwalde.de

Opening hours: Tuesday - Thursday
10am - 12pm and 1pm - 5pm
Saturday
1pm - 5pm
Sunday
10am - 12pm and 2pm - 5pm

Visits outside of our opening hours can also be arranged.
Please register guided tours through the permanent
exhibition and the former camp cemetery well in
advance.

Luckenwalde

THIS PROJECT IS CO-FINANCED BY THE
EUROPEAN UNION

Literature on Stalag III A:

Uwe Mai
Kriegsgefangen in Brandenburg
Stalag III A in Luckenwalde
1939 - 1945

Herbert Bauer
Stalag III A das ehemalige
Kriegsgefangenenlager des
Zweiten Weltkrieges bei
Luckenwalde

Dying in the Stalag

Stalag III A was placed under quarantine at the beginning
of December 1941. It lasted until March/April 1942.
During this period neither Soviet prisoners were accepted
nor could they be sent to other stalags. According
to information from the Supreme Command of the
Armed Forces on the stalag occupancy figures from this
period, it is assumed that the "outgoing patients" were
only death. These figures indicate that nearly 2,000 to
2,500 Soviet prisoners died during the winter of 1941/1942;
this averaged out to a one prisoner per hour. Detailed
information is not available because the monthly reports
of the Supreme Command of the Armed Forces reported
only the occupancy figures from the beginning of the
month, and the reports from the medical service for the
Military District III or the infirmary reports (incoming
and outgoing patients) for this period are very incomplete.
The dead were buried in the Stalag cemetery in mass
graves. The Soviet prisoners in the spring of 1942 were
still being used for work, but only to a limited extent,
because they needed to first regain their strength.

The infirmary was located outside of the prison camp near the cemetery.
All prisoners, including those in the prison garden, were buried here in an unmarked basin. Aerial photo 1945.

The mortality of the Soviet prisoners was extraordinarily
high, especially in comparison to the other nationalities.
The causes of death of non-Soviet prisoners were
varied, however the majority died of infectious diseases,
in particular tuberculosis. There were individual cases
in the death certificates raising unnatural deaths. They
included suicide; shot during an escape attempt or
death due to an injury or an accident while working.
Prisoners were also beaten at interrogation, however
determining to what extent this happened is difficult
to document.

The previous pages were taken from Kate's memories written in the 1980s and 1990s.

Following Kates death in 2017 the family found a further notebook amongst her belongings entitled "Thoughts". Written, again in her ever-neat handwriting, between the years 2004 to 2008. In this, she reflects more deeply on her feelings and relationship with her family in the form of jottings written at random.

These notes, which give a further insight into her character, are transcribed on the following pages.

2004

20 years on my own now - dare I say it - they have been the happiest years of my life. Why? Well, I've been liberated and can now live my own life, not as expected by other people.

My early days were spent in fear of my Father who could never really understand me and expected too much of me - obviously the result of being an only child. If only my Mother's miscarriage had not happened when I was about five years old things might have been very different and I would not have become a bundle of nerves through aiming at the perfection expected of me. Piano, violin and singing lessons, none of which I enjoyed, and a very lonely life with a lovely Mother who was a doormat, devoted to her husband, but whose life was centred around me.

I could never explain to anyone that for my whole life I was scared of War, (maybe because I was born in the middle of one in 1916) but the irrational fear was always with me, firstly when it was suggested that my Father would maybe be called up at the time of the Spanish Civil War in 1936 then having to endure 6 years of trouble 1939-45. Thinking that the worst of my fears were over, then came the Cuba crisis when I feared for my children's lives with threats of nuclear destruction. Later, World Wide crisis left me worrying that my son would be called up, but when I tried to explain my fears to Eddie I was scoffed at so had to keep my anxieties to myself.

In 1938 I drifted into married life because Eddie and I had always been together from a very young age and rarely went anywhere without each other but nobody had any idea that I so nearly changed my mind a few minutes before I was due at the Church. If only I could have seen into the future!

T.A. mobilisation due to the Munich crisis just a few weeks after our wedding was not the best start for married life. It taught me that I would always take second place to the Army, soon to be proved a year later when War was declared.

Admittedly after so many years of doing everything together Eddie made plans for me to be a "Camp follower", having me nearby wherever he was stationed in Britain - good fun really as I travelled and stayed in very odd places for over a year, living in hotels, empty houses and with unknown people, actually ending up in the cottage at Wonersh near Guildford in 1940.

Of course one kind of life ended in 1941 when, after at last becoming pregnant, his second overseas draft shook us rather badly and from then on I had to be strong and very independent, moving back to Carpenders Park, bringing up a child on my own during very frightening times, not knowing where Eddie was, or even if he was alive for many months, then having no idea if we would ever be together again as he was by then a POW and we could not imagine how the War would end as prospects were very bleak at times.

When he finally returned in May 1945 I had to accept that he was a very different man to the one I married and had obviously been affected mentally by the years of captivity; in fact life was very difficult as he expected me to be the Kath he had left behind in 1941, instead of which I had been through a very rough time over the years, something that he did not want to know about. Anything that had happened while he was away did not interest him at all, in fact if I tried to tell him all he would say was "Well, you're here now!"

From then on I realised how selfish he had become and did my best to appease him, putting up with the shock of our move to Bedford without being consulted and then the return of the old restlessness after five years on the farm as he could not settle to working for someone else after years as the "Big Chief" as a Sergeant Major.

So began the quest for self-employment and one of the unhappiest stages of my life - 36 years of hard toil and financial worries with the L.S.A.

Once again I took second place, this time to the land. My parents were shocked and disgusted at the life I was living - the house I was having to put up with and the extremely hard work, especially with three young children to look after.

I think I succeeded in convincing people that all was well and that the way of life was grand but in fact there were times when I was in

absolute despair and felt I couldn't carry on much longer but stuck it out as my upbringing made me accept that I had pledged "for better, for worse, for richer, for poorer, in sickness and in health."

Throughout our 46 years together I did my best to make life for him reasonably satisfactory as I felt so sorry for the terrible time he had spent as a POW but feel that things could have been made easier if only he had told me what his life had been like and not bottled up all his terrible experiences.

Spending 24 hours every day together was not the best way of living as he became such a recluse which is why I took on the part-time job at Penningtons to help out financially and, as you had all left home to live your own lives, give me a more social life but even this was wrong as he decided to do less work on the holding because I was not there to help him all the time.

People used to say that they couldn't believe the way he often seemed to forget that I was his wife and ordered me about as though he employed me. In fact they used to say no employee would have put up with his attitude.

Well, I must be tough as I'm still going strong at 88, have regained my self-confidence and self esteem and have a family to be proud of even though you have sometimes caused problems but I'm grateful to you all for all that you have done for me to help make my life so contented.

There are parts of my wartime life that were frightening but I have tried to forget the unpleasant times - suppose in a way bottled it up like Eddie did but fear that people might think I had joined the "tall story club" if I tried to recall those 6 years.

One of the reasons why I am so contented is that I was able to choose for myself where I would live as twice previously I had no choice when changes were to be made. I saw the old cottage in Bedfordshire only once before we moved - was promised that the renovations to be carried out would make it an attractive home but it was always a very old inconvenient place in the middle of a cow field.

The next move was even worse, a small cramped house, so difficult in which to bring up a young family, that shocked my parents when they saw it so much that they never came there to visit again during the 36 years I was there.

No matter, that's all in the past and my pleasure now in my present circumstances helps me to forget the horrors and disappointments of the past.

I do sometimes think of the future though - hopefully many years ahead yet as I'm aiming for 100 - but I will be extremely angry when I die as I will miss so much of your future lives - just can't imagine not being here to share things with you!

THOUGHTS

I Wish:

- I had not been an only child

- I knew what my family really think about me

- I had been more like my Mother than my Father

- I had been allowed to train for nursing - not put into well paid but boring office work

- I wish I had learned to play the saxophone

Reflections

- the army taught me to live without my husband

- those who are the most non-demonstrative are the ones who care the most (so true)

- give your children wings so they can fly away, and roots so that they know they can return

2008

How can I ever express my gratitude for all that "my family" have done for me and meant to me since 1984 - no fussing but always being there to help me live such a happy and contented life.

In the previous years I had stuck by the promise of "for better, for worse" - very hard at times but I managed to live through it, none the worse for it, I hope, but it was very tough at times, living a hard life that I could never have anticipated, but after the ghastly years Ed had endured as a POW I appreciated that he needed to live a life just as he wanted or completely crack up so I backed him up both physically and financially although not always agreeing with his plans.

****

I have sometimes been asked if I was ever scared during the War years. It's difficult to explain to people that those 6 years became part of our lives; we just learned to live from day to day, not knowing what to expect and trying to live our lives as normal as possible. Don't forget that it happened when I was between the ages of 23-29.

I watched exciting aerial "dog fights" between the RAF and German fighter planes and dreaded the sound of air raid sirens but I think the only things that really scared me were the flying bombs (V1s). When their engines cut out we counted up to 10 before hearing them explode. This was not very pleasant but the nearest to our bungalow at Carpenders Park fell over a mile away and only blew out my light fittings.

One day a shell cap hit the roof, making a lot of noise but only damaging a few tiles, and another time a string of fire bombs fell along the road but just missed me.

When night time air raids were close John Thompson from across the road would come to fetch me, I would wrap Jill up and we would join John's wife and son, Mungo, under the bed. He once said that the funniest sight was to see us all safely protecting our heads but leaving our rear ends stuck up in the air!

****

There have been some memorable events in my long lifetime, excluding personal and family "specials":

- Hearing the wireless for the first time in 1922/3 via a home-made crystal set. Children's Hour with Uncle Mac was the first programme I heard

- Seeing the airship R101 overhead in Leytonstone prior to its fateful crash

- Many years later seeing Halley's Comet night after night

- The excitement of seeing the New Century in on Millennium Night

- But I think the most exciting and awesome event was standing in Honfleur, France to see the total eclipse of the sun. Something I will never forget, almost reducing me to tears

EXPLANATORY INFORMATION

[4]The Death March

The Death March (more accurately known as The Long March) took place during the final months of the Second World War. As the Soviet army advanced on Poland the Nazis made the decision to evacuate the POW camps to prevent the liberation of the prisoners by the Russians. The months of January and February 1945 were amongst the coldest winter months of the 20th century in Europe, with blizzards and temperatures as low as -25 degrees centigrade. Most PoWs were ill prepared for the evacuation, having suffered years of poor rations and wearing clothes ill suited to the appalling weather conditions.

In addition to the risk of freezing or starving to death the prisoners also suffered from exhaustion and diseases such as pneumonia, diphtheria and typhus which they were unable to fight in their exhausted and starving state.

There was also the added danger of being attacked from the air by Allied forces mistaking the POWs for retreating columns of German troops.

It was later estimated that a large number of POWs had marched over 500 miles by the time they were liberated.

Somehow, and Kate wondered how until her dying day, Eddie realised that the Long March would be fraught with these dangers and managed to escape to find his own way home. All she knows is that he returned carrying a kitbag full of dirty Russian roubles, so it appears he may have been helped by Soviet soldiers. As was so often the case with servicemen traumatised by war he never spoke about his experiences. But she did gather that, as a senior NCO, he was not permitted to join the working parties that lower ranks were sent on from the camp. Instead he spent his time studying books about farming and horticulture. This ignited his desire to one day have some land of his own, an achievement realised when he took over the Land Settlement smallholding.

In June 2005, in her quest to discover more about Eddie's journey home, Kate joined a pilgrimage to Lamsdorf in Silesia (now part of Poland) - where Eddie had been imprisoned - organised by the Royal British Legion. This was funded by the National Lottery under the Heroes Return scheme. Kate paid for Judy to accompany her and with others, including surviving veterans and families, they visited the site of the camp but there was little evidence of what had been there six decades earlier. All that was left was woodland and a few ruined buildings. However there was a museum nearby which gave them a clearer picture of the very basic conditions under which the prisoners were kept.

Despite speaking to many of the veterans on the pilgrimage Kate was no nearer to finding out how Eddie made his way home to England. It will remain as one of life's mysteries.

The whole experience of the trip, which was filmed by a team from the BBC as part of their commemorations for the 60th anniversary of the end of the War, appeared to lay a few ghosts to rest, although no answers were found.

The Land Settlement Association

The Association was a U.K. Government scheme set up in 1934 with help from the Plunket Foundation and Carnegie Trust charities to re-settle unemployed workers from depressed industrial areas, mainly in the North East of England. Twenty six such settlements were established in England in the pre-war years.

The estates were set up in rural areas where each successful applicant's family would be given a smallholding of approximately 5 acres, livestock and a newly built cottage. The holdings were grouped in communities which were expected to run agricultural production as co-operative market gardens, with materials bought and produce sold exclusively through the Association.

By the time Eddie took over his holding on the Low Fulney estate in 1950 the scheme was still run as a co-operative, but tenants came from all backgrounds rather than from distressed industrial areas, although several of the older residents were the originals from the North East mining towns and spoke with strong friendly 'Geordie' accents.

The holdings were all sold off when the Land Settlement scheme was wound up in 1983, amongst talk of corruption and mismanagement, which ended in a court case finally resolved in 1991. In the years since, many of the holdings have become specialist plant nurseries or have been converted to paddocks and livery stables. The houses have been modernised and many sold off as private residences.

EPILOGUE

Kate somewhat skipped through the memory of 36 years of her life from her mid-thirties to her late 60s as though they hardly existed. In a way she wished this was true. These were the years spent on the Land Settlement smallholding. Years of hard work, poverty and isolation. The Good Life it was not!

Raising three children and working long hours on the land and in the glasshouses whilst living with a husband who was totally changed from the man she married meant that life was not easy for her. He often seemed to forget that she was his wife and ordered her about as if he employed her. She did her best to make life reasonably satisfactory for him as she felt sorry for the time he had spent as a POW but felt things could have been made easier if he'd told her what his life had been like, and not bottled up all his terrible experiences.

With Dad being a recluse and them living and working together 24 hours a day it took its toll on her. When we, the children, became independent, Mum grasped the chance to take on a part-time job at Penningtons fashion shop in Spalding. As well as helping out financially this opportunity provided a social life for her, at last forming friendships outside the small world of the Land Settlement. Mum spread her wings and broadened her outlook even further by volunteering as a receptionist each Tuesday evening at Spalding Family Planning Clinic. These moves did not please Dad who showed less incentive to work on the holding because she was not there to help him all the time.

In the early 1980s, thanks to the Land Settlement scheme finally being wound up, the opportunity arose for Dad to purchase the smallholding. Sadly, at around the same time, he was diagnosed with cancer and passed away at home, at the age of 71, in early

1984. Although, as commonplace in those unenlightened times, Mums name had not been on the tenancy agreement, completion of the purchase did finally go ahead, allowing her to sell the holding and start the next stage of her life as an active widow.

It was at this time she announced that she wished to be known as Kate. For all of her life, she'd been called Kath, short for Kathleen, but never having liked this because, she said, "it sounds like a greasy spoon café".

She purchased a bungalow a few miles away in Weston, just five doors down the road from my sister Jill. Here she spent 25 happy years tending her garden and regularly seeing her family who all lived within 5 miles of her. In addition to looking after her house and garden, she would drive her Mini Metro into Spalding, to help out at the St  Barnabas Hospice charity shop, where she became the team leader. Volunteering for this cancer charity was in recognition of Eddie's final illness and because Jill had been successfully treated for breast cancer a couple of years earlier.

Widowhood allowed Kate the opportunity to indulge in her love of travel, in Britain, Ireland and to more unusual holiday destinations such as Bulgaria, Poland and Czechoslovakia. These were usually low budget coach holidays, either travelling alone, accompanied by  Jill or myself, or sometimes with a work colleague. Her biggest adventure was when she travelled alone, shortly after Eddies death, to visit his sister Joan in New Zealand. Whilst there she toured the North Island and flew home via the United States, thus having flown right round the world. At the age of 94, still bright mentally but frail physically, she had a fall at home and broke her femur. She continued living alone in her bungalow for a further two years with assistance from her family, but the time came when it was apparent that she needed full-time care and so spent her final years in a nearby care home.

 The steely determination and independence she had shown in her earlier life were obviously still there, though, because she carried on living for a further five years. She achieved her ambition of reaching her 100th birthday which was spent surrounded by family members including Kate's five great-grandchildren who all affectionately called her Nanna Kate. Sadly Jill had died of lung cancer the previous year at the age of 73 having suffered from several health issues over the years.

On September the 17th 2017, at the grand age of 101, Kate passed away peacefully during the night. A long eventful life drawn to a close, the last of a generation who, due to the War, gave up their best years for our future, for which we must all be grateful.

Scrapbook

Acknowledgements

Spring and summer 2020, which will be remembered as the year of the Coronavirus, was an unusual time for all of us. It was a time of reflection and a time to reassess our priorities. Like many, I had previously been caught up in a whirlpool of being busy simply for the sake of being busy. Then, all at once, I had time to do things for myself. Things that I wanted to do. The first of these was to re-read Mums memories which had been stored in a box since her death almost three years previously. Now was the time to write the book of her life.

I wish to express my thanks to Nigel Battley of Bats Publications Ltd for putting this random collection of jottings and photographs in a semblance of order which has made this book into an interesting and readable piece of family and social history.

Sincere thanks must also go to my husband, Mike, for all of his encouragement in making sure I finally went ahead with this project instead of just talking about it.

Thanks, also, to my brother for checking through the writings and making one or two corrections.

Of course, extra special thanks must go to Mum for providing the material for this book. I'm sure she would be delighted to know that her writing will be there for future generations of her family to read.

I have compiled this anthology from the books and papers she saved over the years. Her collection of memories, along with newspaper cuttings and correspondence with various organisations such as the BBC have made for fascinating reading, and have given me further insight to the woman who was simply "Mum" to Jill, my brother and myself.

It is a celebration of her life as well as a history lesson to her direct descendants, which at the time of writing - in the midst of the Corona Virus Pandemic, Summer 2020 – are her two surviving children - my brother and myself, our children and grandchildren. Those grandchildren being my two sons and my brother's two daughters. Between them, they gave Mum five great-grandchildren all born in the New Millennium.

My sister Jill (1941-2015) sadly predeceased Mum.

Just think. If Mum had chickened out of her wedding to Dad - which she almost did at the last minute - none of us would have existed!

Thanks Mum.

Judy Chapman (nee Cooper)
June 2020

Forever in our hearts

"A treasured item of Jewellery"

made by Kathleen's Maternal Grandfather
William Grimshaw (pg. 2)